# Basic Car Maintenance for Women

## An Essential Guide and How-To for Your Car

Jessy Patterson

Basic Car Maintenance for Women: An Essential Guide and How-To for Your Car

Copyright © Jessy Patterson, 2007 – 2009
Cover art and design copyright © Jessy Patterson, 2009
All rights reserved.

Summary: A basic car maintenance guide and how-to written with women in mind, offering foundations in engine oil, fuel systems, tires, and hoses and belts. Includes a special section on jumper cable set-up and safety.

Reference/Handbook & Manuals
ISBN 1-4392-3031-5

No part of this work may be reproduced or transmitted in any form or by any means, electronic or mechanical, including photocopying and recording, or by any information storage or retrieval system without the prior written permission of Jessy Patterson unless such copying is expressly permitted by federal copyright law. Images contained within this document are the property of Microsoft Office Clipart or Jessy Patterson, unless otherwise noted in the References section of this manual. Address inquiries to jessypatterson@yahoo.com

Every attempt has been made to ensure that all information presented in this manual is correct and accurate; no liability can be accepted by the author or current or future publishers for losses, damages or injury caused by any errors in, or omissions from, the given information.

Printed in the U.S.A.

All brand and product names mentioned in this manual are trademarks or registered trademarks of their respective holders, including the following: Chevrolet, Chevy, Holley, Edelbrock, Flowmaster, BF Goodrich, Powerblocktv.com, Speed Channel, Booster-In-A-Bag by Coleman Cable Systems, Inc, Microsoft Word, Microsoft Word Clipart, Google.com, Jeep, Dodge.

This book is dedicated to my mom.

And in loving memory of Grandpa Murfin.

# Table of Contents

**INTRODUCTION** ........................................................................................................... 1
**GETTING STARTED** ..................................................................................................... 5
   THE RIGHT TOOLS ....................................................................................................... 5
      *What you will need* ................................................................................................. 5
         The Essentials ..................................................................................................... 6
**BASIC CAR MAINTENANCE CHECKS AND TASKS** ............................................... 7
   OPTIMAL HEALTH ....................................................................................................... 7
      *Engine Oil* ................................................................................................................ 7
         Checking the oil level ......................................................................................... 8
         Adding Engine oil .............................................................................................. 9
      *Fuel System* ........................................................................................................... 10
         Checking/Changing the Air Filter .................................................................... 11
      *Tires* ....................................................................................................................... 12
         Performing the 'One-Cent' Check ................................................................... 14
         Assessing tire wear and tear ............................................................................. 14
         Checking tire pressure ..................................................................................... 15
         Adding air to tires ............................................................................................ 16
      *Hoses and Belts* .................................................................................................... 17
         Performing the Touch-Feel Check – Serpentine belt ..................................... 18
         Performing the Touch-Feel Check – Hoses .................................................... 19
         Performing the Look-Listen Check – Serpentine belt and hoses .................. 19
**EXTRAS** ...................................................................................................................... 20
   MORE ESSENTIALS .................................................................................................... 20
      *Windshield Wipers* ............................................................................................... 20
      *Jumper Cables* ...................................................................................................... 22
         Jumper cable safety precautions ..................................................................... 24
         Using jumper cables ........................................................................................ 25
      *Maintenance Log – Sample Sheet* ........................................................................ 27
**GLOSSARY** ................................................................................................................ 28
**GENERAL REFERENCES AND RESOURCES** ........................................................ 29
**INDEX** ........................................................................................................................ 30

# Basic Car Maintenance for Women

## Introduction

I love cars. Actually, to be more specific, I love what's under the hood. Engines with quality performance parts or just old school reliability get my motor running – pun intended. Give me an old Chevy truck with a big-block, throw in a four-barrel Holley® carb, Edelbrock® intake, Flowmaster® exhaust and a set of BF Goodrich® All-terrains and I am the happiest woman on the block. You know what I mean? OK, so you may not have any idea what I am talking about. Possibly, the only words you recognize are Chevy and BF Goodrich®. But don't worry. You may have no desire to spend your Saturday afternoon changing your car's oil, and sitting through an hour or two on the PowerBlock station would be more like torture to you than entertainment. Don't worry, I won't ask you to change your own oil or watch re-runs on the PowerBlock station. But it is my love of cars and engines that prompted me to write this manual. I have changed my own oil, spark plugs, spark plug wires, differential fluid, and done numerous other maintenance tasks all with a smile on my face. While my appreciation for vehicles is deep-rooted and sincere, I appreciate that not everyone shares my interest and certainly not to the extent that I do. I also recognize that women typically shy away from vehicles and any maintenance associated for varying reasons. I can appreciate that there are women who are just not the do-it-yourself type. At the same time, I know there are women who are curious and are either slightly uncertain or very confident that they could do some car maintenance if they only knew what to check, when to check it, and how to go about it. But you may not be fully committed to getting downright dirty in the process. If you are one of these women, keep reading.

Basic car maintenance knowledge and know-how is not elusive. It's not mysterious. It's learned, plain and simple. And yes, you can do it, even if the only maintenance you have performed thus far is putting gasoline in your tank and filling your windshield washer fluid.

If you can drive a car, you can maintain it. You should want to, considering it gets you from point A to point B pretty consistently, and you'd probably like it to continue to do so.

What will this manual teach you and what will it cover? Let me first tell you what it will **not** cover. It will not cover any maintenance to carbureted engines, diesel engines, alternative fuel or hybrid vehicles. If you aren't sure whether your vehicle is carbureted, check your Owner's Manual. Also, know that all vehicles built and manufactured after 1990 have electronic fuel injection systems. Electronic fuel injection replaced the carbureted engine. Obviously, diesel engines and alternative fuel engines require specific fuel sources. A vehicle that is termed a hybrid usually implies that it is partially powered by electricity. This manual will also not contain a breakdown of all parts and pieces of an engine.

Is this manual for you? It is if you own a vehicle manufactured after 1990 or one that contains an electronic fuel injection system and is not described as one of the previously mentioned vehicles. It is also for you if you want to learn a little bit more about your car and how to keep it running smoothly and maybe save some time and money along the way. It is for you if you are a self-reliant woman who is smart enough to utilize the car services available to her, such as oil changes and tire rotation, and also smart enough to recognize that there are necessary maintenance and safety checks that are either not available as service checks or too inconvenient and costly to have someone else perform. Those same safety and maintenance checks are easy and cheap to do yourself.

Alright, so, what *is* it that this manual will teach you? Well, just as the title suggests, it will teach the basics. The basics include checking your engine oil level, changing the air filter, checking tire pressure and assessing tire tread wear, checking hoses and belts within the engine, replacing windshield wipers and adding washer fluid, and using jumper cables. This guide is intended to accompany your car's Owner's Manual. But unlike your Owner's Manual, this guide will give you a foundation to help you understand the systems and functions of your car and why regular maintenance is important to your safety and the overall health of your car. It will also provide you with step-by-step instruction to perform these maintenance tasks.

So, what do you need to know before you get started? Probably not much you don't already know. You will need to know how to open the hood of your car and be able to locate parts that are labeled within your engine. Why don't you do that now? Go ahead. Take this book out to your car, pop the hood, and have a good look.

At first glance, you might think that it looks like a collection of metal parts and wires all jumbled together in a configuration only a mechanic could comprehend. But look closer. Someone was thinking of you when they put all of those pieces and parts together. Notice the color-coding and labeling on some of the caps and covers. You should see a color theme. Locate these color-coded and/or labeled parts: Engine oil filler cap, engine oil dipstick, and washer fluid reservoir. (Refer to Figure 1 for an example of these parts within the engine bay). Did you find all of the parts? Were they all labeled and/or color-coded? Guess what? Car manufacturers did that on purpose. All of those parts are labeled and color-coded because the manufacturer intended you to perform maintenance checks on those specific parts and systems. Yellow is most often used to associate these parts, but your car may have red instead. You will learn more about the contents of your engine as we delve into the related chapters.

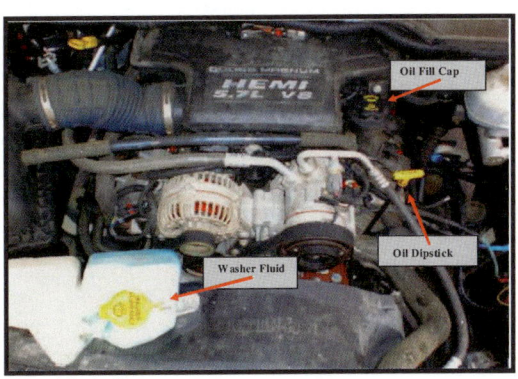

Figure 1 Engine Bay

How do you feel about your engine now? Are you at least a little intrigued? Maybe even a little surprised to find these parts labeled and color-coded—just for you? Do you feel like you could 'hang with the boys'? Maybe not just yet, but we're getting there. Being able to 'hang with the boys' isn't my intention here, but you might consider it an added bonus.

You have to admit that acquiring knowledge about something you undoubtedly use everyday is satisfying. And it can't hurt to know a little bit more about one of the most expensive items in your possession.

But hold on. Before we 'put the pedal to the metal' there are a few more things you need to know about this guide. First, I urge you to read through each section and the how-to steps before you perform any type of maintenance, preferably while in the company of your car. Locate the parts and areas on which you will be performing maintenance. Familiarize yourself with your vehicle and your engine. Look through your Owner's Manual and familiarize yourself with it and the sections and topics it includes. This guide is intended to accompany your Owner's Manual. Throughout this guide you will notice italicized words and terms. Those words and terms are included in the *Glossary* section for easy reference.

I have made every effort to ensure that this guide is educational, easy-to-use, and non-intimidating. It is my sincere hope that you are able to complete the maintenance tasks and will gain a sense of accomplishment from doing so. There is supreme power in knowing you can identify engine parts, and check your oil level and tire pressure, all while wearing cute shoes and lipstick, if you so choose.

# Getting Started

## The Right Tools

### What You Will Need

**M**aintaining a car is hard work. It is harder still if you don't have the right tools to help you along the way. In this section, we will discover the proper tools needed to help you keep your car running smoothly.

The most important tool in your bag will be your Owner's Manual. If you don't know what this is, check the glove box. When you purchased (or leased) your car, it should have come equipped with this essential guide. In most cases, it comes sheathed in a vinyl case that also contains your warranty book and a maintenance logbook. If you purchased your car used from a dealership or from a previous owner, you may not have this manual. But don't fret; there are ways of obtaining one. The cheapest way is to check at your local library. You should also check with the dealerships in your area as they may have copies on hand or be able to direct you to their supplier. The Internet is another option, though you will want to be cautious there. Some sites may lead you to a maintenance manual for your particular make and model car, but not all models are the same, and there may be some key differences in what each model requires in terms of maintenance.

In addition to your Owner's Manual, there are other tools that you may already have on hand. When checking fluid levels and cleaning parts you will need to have clean rags, old shirts, or towels. Many retail auto parts stores and even discount superstores sell bags-of-rags, specifically for the purposes of car maintenance and repair. This is a convenient and easy way to ensure that you have clean rags on hand when performing maintenance checks. While not always necessary, gloves are useful when handling oil and other engine fluids. They can protect your hands from unnecessary scratches and cuts and just keep you cleaner in general. Cloth gloves are the most durable and cost-effective, if you choose to wear them. You will find a list of the essential items on the following page.

**THE ESSENTIALS**

- Car Owner's Manual
- Maintenance Log (Sample sheet on page 27)
- Clean rags/towels
- Protective gloves
- Funnel
- Screwdrivers: Phillips and flathead
- First-Aid Kit
- Tire gauge
- Pliers
- Motor oil/Engine oil
- Air filter
- Wire brush
- Washer fluid
- Protective goggles
- Step-stool or short ladder
- Jumper cables

# Basic Car Maintenance Checks and Tasks

OPTIMAL HEALTH

## ENGINE OIL

Maintaining the engine oil is fairly straightforward and simple. But don't mistake this maintenance task as unimportant. It is far from it. In fact, engine oil takes its place, in terms of importance, at the top of the list with gasoline a very close second.

You may know that you need to change your oil every 3000-6000 miles. You may even be aware that there is an *oil filter* and *dipstick* housed within your car's engine. But what you may not know is that your car and engine are so dependent on proper oil maintenance that, if unattended, your engine can and will become damaged beyond repair. Think of your engine's oil as you would blood. If blood becomes contaminated or infected and is left untreated, the body will shut down, ultimately leading to death. Your engine functions the same way with respect to the oil. Fortunately, this maintenance check is easy to perform, once you know the When and How. Checking your engine's oil should be a weekly task.

You have probably seen drivers performing this at a gas station while filling up. Or perhaps you have seen a gas station attendant performing the same task. Neither is preferred for several reasons. First, the oil should be relatively cool, or better, it should be cold, when you check it. Even if you have only been driving for 10 minutes, your engine is no longer cool. The engine needs to be off for more than 5 minutes before it is safe and useful to perform the check. Ideally, the oil should have the opportunity to return to the oil pan for an optimal reading and a level surface is preferred when performing this check.

> **WARNING:** Engine oil, like any cooking oil, can become hot enough to burn your skin and cause permanent damage. Never check, change, or add oil while the engine is running.

For the most accurate reading, check your oil in the morning when the vehicle has sat overnight and the engine is cold, and while the vehicle is parked on a level surface. Perform the oil level check once a week.

Jessy Patterson

## CHECKING THE OIL LEVEL

> **NOTES:**
> ▪ You will need a clean, lint-free rag, old shirt, or towel on which to wipe the oil. You should also consider wearing protective gloves.
> ▪ Check your Owner's Manual for a diagram of your vehicle's engine and the location of the oil dipstick, if you are at all uncertain.

1. Locate the engine oil dipstick.

> **NOTE:** The dipstick is typically located along one side of the engine, toward the front or back. It has a looped handle or handle ring. In most vehicles less than 20 years old, the dipstick handle is color-coded and labeled for easier visibility. Do not confuse the oil dipstick with the transmission dipstick! If they are color-coded they will be the same color, but each should be labeled.

2. Pull the oil dipstick out and using your rag, wipe the end clean.

3. Replace the dipstick, being careful not to force it. The dipstick should slide relatively easily back into place. If it does not, turn it around and try again.

4. Now, pull the dipstick back out. At the end of the dipstick you will see markings, such as ADD and FULL or SAFE and crosshatch or arrow markings.

5. Determine the highest level of oil on the dipstick.

    a. If the oil film appears to only reach the ADD mark you will need to add oil. One quart of oil should bring the level back up to the FULL mark if the oil film is currently at the top of the ADD mark.

    b. If the oil film is below the ADD mark you may need two or more quarts.

    c. If the oil film is in between the ADD and FULL marks, you do not need to add oil, doing so could damage your engine.

    d. If the oil film is at or near the FULL mark your check is complete.

6. Replace the dipstick when your check is complete.

> **NOTE:** When checking the oil level, take note of any suspicious odor or consistency. If the oil smells like gasoline, you should have the oil changed immediately. If the oil appears dirty or unusually thick, it is also time for an oil change.

## ADDING ENGINE OIL

**NOTES:**

- There are several types and varying grades of engine oil. Your Owner's Manual should indicate which oil is best suited for your vehicle. Also, many vehicles have this information printed on the oil fill cap.

- You will need a funnel when adding oil to prevent spilling. If the oil spills onto the engine, you may see smoke coming off the engine when you next turn the car on or drive it.

1. Locate and remove the *oil filler* cap. It is usually located near the oil dipstick.

2. Based on your oil level check, add approximately one-half quart of oil at a time to the oil filler hole, checking the oil level after about one-half quart to avoid overfilling.

**WARNING:** Be careful not to overfill the engine oil. Adding too much oil can cause result in serious damage to your engine. It is important to keep close a watch on the oil level when adding engine oil.

3. Replace the oil filler cap when the oil level reaches the FULL mark on the dipstick.

## FUEL SYSTEM

As you may have guessed, the fuel system is what makes your car go. But did you know that your car also needs air? Fuel and air mix in the fuel injection system to make your car go. In this section, we will cover the parts of an *electronic fuel injection* system and how the system works. Later, you will learn how to check and change the *air filter*.

As you know, you add gas to the gas tank. This is also known as the *fuel tank*. A pump, called a *fuel pump*, pumps the fuel from the *fuel tank* into the *fuel lines* and then into the *fuel injectors*. A computer in your car's engine controls all of this electronically. The fuel injection system is responsible for maintaining the proper mixture of fuel and air. It injects the mixture into the car's cylinders or combustion chamber. There are two types of electronic fuel injection (EFI): *throttle body* and *multi-port*.

Throttle body injection replaced the *carburetor*. In this system, the fuel/air mixture is combined in the car's throttle. Rather than using individual fuel injectors, the throttle body system may use *injection nozzles* to distribute the fuel/air mixture to the cylinders, controlled by a solenoid, which is a mechanical device regulated by the electrical system.

In a multi-port injection system, the fuel/air mixture is performed in the *intake port* and distributed through individual fuel injectors to each cylinder. The intake port contains a valve, called the *intake valve* that allows the air and fuel to combine before being distributed to the fuel injectors.

Both the throttle body and multi-port systems also contain a *fuel filter* and air filter. As their names suggest, these devices filter the fuel and the air before the two are combined and injected into the cylinders.

The fuel injection system is a delicate and complex one as the parts are controlled electronically. Maintenance is better left to the professionals. However, you may be able to perform two tasks: checking and changing the air filter. In most cases, the air filter may only need to be replaced once per year. But your driving environment should also be considered. You may need to check or change the air filter more or less frequently depending on where you live and drive. For example, if you frequently travel or live on a dirt road, your filter can become overloaded or full of debris more quickly than someone who frequently travels on paved, relatively clean and well-maintained stretches of road. Check the air filter at least once per year and more often if your driving environment requires it.

> **WARNING:** Your Owner's Manual will indicate how often the air filter should be cleaned depending on the type of filter your car requires. The manual should also indicate if cleaning or changing the air filter should be done professionally. As cars have become more advanced and complicated, and the engines more compact, it may be difficult to access the filter. Some cars also require more precision in the placement of the filter due to the electronic sensors that make up the fuel system. Check your Owner's Manual and proceed with caution!

## CHECKING/CHANGING THE AIR FILTER

> **CAUTION:** The engine should remain off while performing this check. Do not attempt to start the engine without the air filter in place.

1. Locate the air cleaner filter also referred to as the air filter. This should be labeled within the engine. The air filter is located inside the casing/housing unit and is a square, pleated, papery device.

2. Remove the casing/housing unit. This may require a Phillips or flat-head screwdriver, or the unit may be held in place by wing nuts or clips.

3. Remove the air filter from within the unit.

4. Check it for excessive debris and dirt by holding it up to a light.

    - If it appears to be clogged or full, it is best to replace it.

    - If it is relatively clean, your check is complete.

5. Return the filter to the housing unit or replace it with a new filter as specified by your Owner's Manual.

6. Return and secure the casing/housing unit.

Jessy Patterson

# TIRES

You know what they are, but many people don't realize how important proper air pressure, tire condition, and tire alignment and rotation are to their safety. While you may not be able to perform all of these tasks on your own, it is important to understand their relevance in terms of safety. This section will provide an overview of these topics and the steps necessary to check tire tread, assess wear and tear, check tire pressure, and add air to tires. Before we get started it is important to mention that the topic of tires is an enormous one. There are entire books dedicated to this topic and include everything from changing a flat tire to the construction of tires. I will only be scratching the surface in this overview. You will find more in-depth and thorough topic sources at your local bookstore or library.

Let's first discuss tire alignment and rotation and their role in driver safety. You have probably at some point or another driven or at least been in a car with poor alignment. The car pulled to the left or right or refused to drive in a straight line when you threw your hands in the air and yelled, "Look, Ma, no hands!" The car or steering wheel may also feel shaky if the alignment is off. Another determiner of poor alignment is uneven tread wear on tires, though this could also be a result of improper tire inflation, but I will get to that in a bit. Clearly, tire alignment affects your driving safety. Fortunately, it is an inexpensive fix, but not one I recommend doing yourself. Leave tire alignment as well as tire rotation to the professionals. Tire rotation is done in order to extend or maximize the life of your tires. There are patterns of rotation depending on your vehicle's drive train, tire size differences, types of tires, and a few other factors. I will not cover these specifics here, but your Owner's Manual should specify the rotation pattern recommended for your vehicle. In terms of maintenance, I recommend taking your vehicle to a reputable mechanic or tire service location twice a year for rotation, tire balancing, and alignment. Many tire service locations offer free rotation, balance, and alignment for the life of your tires if they were purchased through their location. Take advantage of this service if it is available to you. It can save you time and money.

As I suggested before, there are countless books and manuals for the topic of tires. If you were beginning to think that tires are high maintenance, you would be correct, but consider what they do on a daily basis. Your tires have a rather heavy burden to bear, not to mention, some pretty tough job responsibilities. They bear the combined weight of you, your passengers, any extra items you or they bring along, and most incredibly, the weight of your entire vehicle and engine. That is pretty impressive. Now consider your daily driving conditions and environment, and add that to their responsibilities. We drive in all sorts of conditions — rain, snow, extreme heat and cold — most of us without a second thought for our tires. Inconsistent climates, temperature changes, seasonal fluctuations, road conditions, stop and go traffic, long trips, and high-speed driving affect not only our daily lives but also that of our cars. All of these factors, whether alone or combined, alter

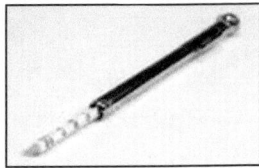

Figure 2 Tire Gauge

the tire pressure and affect wear and tear on your tires. That is why it is important to perform regular checks for tire tread wear and proper tire inflation. Fortunately, both of these do-it-yourself maintenance tasks are cheap.

Before you get started though, you will need your tire gauge to check the tire pressure. So make sure you have it handy. See Figure 2 above for an example of a tire gauge.

While you perform the tire tread and wear and tear assessment, note the tire specification information listed on each tire and the tire pressure requirement for the front and rear tires listed on the Certification Label. The Certification Label is specific to your vehicle and is located inside the driver's side door or doorjamb, the glove box, and sometimes the trunk. The maximum *psi* (pounds per square inch) listed on the tires is not necessarily the required psi for your vehicle. See Figure 3 above for location of maximum air inflation (psi). Refer to your Owner's Manual if you have trouble locating the Certification Label. Let's move on now to the tire tread and assessment.

Figure 3 Max PSI info

Jessy Patterson

13

Abraham Lincoln is probably best known for the Gettysburg Address; he is lesser known for his ability to ascertain tire tread wear, but it's all in his head, on a penny that is. The 'one-cent' check (described below) is quick and cheap, but very valuable. It can help determine when new tires are needed. Use your maintenance log to keep track of tread changes and the frequency of your checks.

## PERFORMING THE 'ONE-CENT' CHECK

1. Using a U.S. penny, insert the edge between the tire tread, Lincoln's head facing down.

   - If the top of Lincoln's head is visible, the tread is worn and the tires may need to be replaced soon.

   - If any or most of Lincoln's head is not visible, the tire tread is still good.

2. Repeat Step 1 for all tires. Be sure to check several sections of tread on each tire.

## ASSESSING TIRE WEAR AND TEAR

**Note:** When assessing wear and tear look for specific wear patterns as they could be the result of improper tire inflation/alignment. Wear on the outside edges may indicate under-inflation. Wear centered on the tire may indicate over-inflation. Wear along one side indicates improper alignment.

1. Examine each tire thoroughly.

   a. Check for cracks along the edges and tire walls.

   b. Check for debris such as stones, nails, glass, sharp objects embedded in the tire, and listen for leaks.

   c. Remove loose debris or stones.

**WARNING:** Do not attempt to remove a nail or other sharp object if it is embedded or if you can hear air leaking from the hole. Take the car immediately to a tire service location for repair or replacement or call a tire service location for assistance, if you are unsure what to do.

2. Check the tread for wear patterns: bald spots, bumps or bulges, cuts and scrapes, soft or mushy areas, and specific wear patterns as noted above.

CHECKING TIRE PRESSURE

NOTE: When checking tire pressure, always perform a cold (air) check, meaning the tires should be cold. The vehicle should be parked for more than 3 hours, before performing the check.

1. Determine the proper inflation for the front and rear tires using the Certification Label on your vehicle.

2. For each tire, locate the tire valve and remove the valve cap. See Figure 4 for Tire Valve example.

3. Place the tire pressure gauge over the valve and press down for the reading.

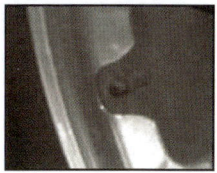

**Figure 4 Tire Valve**

- A small stick will release from the end of the gauge for the reading. Ensure that you are not covering the end of the tire gauge with your hand or fingers.

- Be sure to push the stick back inside the tire gauge before the next reading.

4. Make a note of the pressure reading for each tire.

- If the pressure is above the maximum requirement per the Certification Label, you can release some air in the tires using the tire gauge by pressing on the stem within the valve or by depressing the stem with your finger or firm object.

CAUTION: Be careful not to release too much air. You will need to take a new reading periodically to make sure you have not released too much air.

- If the air pressure is below the required psi, you will need to add air.

5. Replace all valve caps once the tire pressure check is complete.

Jessy Patterson

## ADDING AIR TO TIRES

NOTE: If you do not have an air compressor at home (most people don't), you will need to take your car to a gas station or service station. Be prepared to pay for the air as most places charge for this service. Also, not all gas stations have air pumps. You may want to locate a gas station or service location prior to performing the tire pressure check, so that you don't waste time and air pressure driving around.

1. Remove the valve cap.

2. You will probably have to pay for the air before the air pump machine turns on.

3. Place the air nozzle over the valve and press down firmly, keeping the air nozzle pressed to the valve as you add air.

4. Make sure you have your notes for each tire and are only adding the difference between your cold air reading and the required psi for each tire.

5. To ensure you have added the proper amount of air to each tire, check the tire pressure periodically.

6. When the tire pressure for each tire reaches the required amount, replace the valve caps.

## Hoses and Belts

**H**oses and belts, while not in the same category in terms of function, are grouped together as part of your engine's accessories. Individually, they perform very different tasks. Hoses are generally the 'connectors' connecting one part to another to perform or complete a single process or job. Belts are the workhorses within the engine. They transfer power from the engine and process movement within the parts of the engine. Though hoses and belts do need to be replaced from time to time, I will not endeavor to advise or instruct in this area. I will focus on condition and preventative maintenance. In this section, you will employ a Look-Listen & Touch-Feel approach to this maintenance check.

As not all engines are the same, not all cars have the same number of hoses or belts. More than likely, your vehicle will have only one belt, called a *serpentine belt*, also known as a drive belt. Refer to Figure 5 on page 18 for an example of the serpentine belt location. For the purposes of this section, I will assume your vehicle has only this belt and several hoses snaked throughout the engine. If you have already examined your engine as I suggested in the Introduction, you have a good idea of the number of hoses and belts within your engine. If you have not taken the opportunity to become familiar with the engine, I urge you to do so now.

> **CAUTION: The engine should be off while you are examining the parts within. As always, practice caution and avoid touching parts, as they may be hot. You will be instructed to turn the engine on when you perform the Look-Listen check.**

You will discover that the hoses within the engine vary in size, shape, length, and appearance. Notice also that the hoses contain connection clamps to maintain their secure connection. The serpentine belt should be located at the front of the engine.

As I mentioned previously, you will be performing a Look-Listen & Touch-Feel maintenance check. However, the order in which you perform these checks will be reversed. For safety purposes and while the engine is off, you will first perform the Touch-Feel check.

## PERFORMING THE TOUCH-FEEL CHECK – SERPENTINE BELT

> **CAUTION:** Before performing the Touch-Feel checks, make sure the engine has had time to cool. Also, when performing this check, do not attempt to pull, lift, or remove the serpentine belt. Note that you will only be able to perform this check on the portion of the belt exposed to you. It is not necessary to touch or feel every inch of the belt. The Look-Listen check will complete the process.

1. With the engine off, pop the hood of the vehicle.

2. Locate the serpentine belt. See Figure 5 for an example.

3. Touch the top and undersides of the belt, feeling the texture with your fingers. The top of the belt will have a smooth texture, while the underside will have ridges or lines (tracks).

4. Check for consistency in the texture on the top and underside of the belt.

    **Figure 5 Serpentine Belt**

    a. Note any rough areas on the top of the belt and smooth or worn areas on the underside.

    b. Check for cracks, cuts and nicks, tears, fraying or chipped edges, and thinning of the belt. If any of these are noted and the belt seems overly damaged, you should have the belt replaced.

5. Without pulling or tugging, feel the tension of the belt. If the belt feels loose, it may also squeak when the Look-Listen check is done. This is a clear sign of a belt that needs to be replaced.

## PERFORMING THE TOUCH-FEEL CHECK – HOSES

1. With the engine still off, locate as many hoses as possible. You may need a stepstool or short ladder to gain full access to the hoses.

2. As you did with the serpentine belt, check for consistency in the texture of the hose. Check for cracks, cuts, holes, brittleness, creases, burns, and loose connection clamps, being careful not to pull or tug on the hoses or clamps.

3. Tighten any loose connections.

4. Repeat Steps 1 through 3 for all accessible hoses.

> **NOTE:** If you notice areas of concern on any hose, look for writing on the hose indicating its purpose, for instance, heater hose. Knowing which hose is damaged will make it easier for a mechanic to locate and replace it.

## PERFORMING THE LOOK-LISTEN CHECK – SERPENTINE BELT AND HOSES

> **WARNING:** Do not attempt to touch or feel anything within the engine while it is running. Keep your hair pulled back and remove or secure any loose or dangling jewelry or clothing. Use your stepstool or ladder, if necessary, to get a good view of the engine, maintaining a safe distance from moving parts.

1. With the hood still open, start the engine.

2. Listen for squeaking or squealing of the serpentine belt and hissing or leaking sounds from any of the hoses.

3. Keep a watchful eye on the hoses. Look for signs of leaks—fluid spitting, spraying or oozing, or steam emissions.

> **NOTE:** Any problems noted with belts and hoses should be addressed and/or replaced by a professional as soon as possible.

Jessy Patterson

# Extras

## More Essentials

### Windshield Wipers

Swish (pause). Swish (pause). Swish (pause). That is the sound you should hear when using these faithful and relentless critters. Thud, thud, thud, thud, thud, as the tortured wiper blade skids across the windshield, is not the sound you should hear. Squeaking and squealing of any sort is also not healthy. But you knew that, right?

It is surprising how infrequently we consider our windshield wipers, especially in terms of safety. But travel anywhere in a downpour with wiper blades that are old or damaged and you won't soon forget how important they are. The windshield wiper blades themselves are an easy fix. And knowing when to replace them is just as simple. When they no longer do the job they were intended to do — that is, wipe the windshield clean — it is time to replace them, once a year is usually sufficient. However, there are factors, such as climate and improper use that can diminish the life expectancy of the blades. Using the wipers to remove ice and snow, or on a dry windshield will, inevitably, cost you new blades more frequently. You can help extend the life of the blades by periodically wiping them clean with a cloth or paper towel.

Buying and replacing wiper blades couldn't be easier. There are numerous retail auto parts stores and other discount retailers to help with this task. The difficult part will be deciding amongst the many types, sizes, brands, and styles of wiper blades. Most retail auto parts stores have either a reference book or computer reference point located in the wiper blade aisle. These are intended as self-help reference points. The reference book or computer will list specifically which blades fit your vehicle based on the make, model, and year. If you are unsure of the proper blade type and size for your vehicle, ask a salesperson to help you. When replacing the blades be sure to follow the instructions on the package. Most blades simply snap into place on the windshield wiper arm. However, there are always some exceptions, so read the instructions carefully.

Now, I cannot leave this chapter without mentioning windshield washer fluid, but we won't spend much time here. Is it considered an essential? Yes, it is. And it is another simple task. The windshield washer fluid is housed under the hood. The clear or white plastic reservoir is clearly labeled as windshield washer fluid. The fluid itself is usually a blue color, though it may be a pink color as well and can be purchased at gas stations, auto parts stores, grocery stores, convenience stores, and discount retail chains to name a few. When the fluid appears low, fill it back up. It really is that simple. There is nothing else to check or change. Just remember to put the cap back on the reservoir and close the hood.

## Jumper Cables

**W**hether you have been in this situation or not, you can imagine the panic and stress created when your car won't start and you find yourself stranded. Hopefully, if this happens to you, you find yourself in a parking lot full of nice people willing to help. Of course, you can't count on that happening. So, as with anything in life, these types of situations are easier to handle if you are prepared. This section will discuss the safety precautions necessary when using jumper cables and will provide the step-by-step instructions for proper jumper cable setup.

If you have not yet purchased jumper cables to keep in your vehicle, I recommend Booster-In-A-Bag made by Coleman Cable Systems, Inc. The convenient bag not only provides a storage area for your cables, but also keeps them safe from the elements and anything else that might be rolling around in your trunk. The best feature of the bag, however, is the easy to use instructions and accompanying pictures printed on the outside of the bag.

As I mentioned at the beginning of this section I will go over the safety precautions you need to be aware of before attempting to jump start a car. A bulleted list will be provided as a recap and for easy reference on page 24, and the step-by-step instructions for proper jumper cable setup will follow on pages 25 and 26.

First, always have your Owner's Manual in your vehicle. You will need to consult it when jump starting your car. Second, remove all jewelry and any clothing with metal fasteners, zippers, etc. Metal can cause a short circuit between electrical contacts. Do not use or leave tools on or near the battery or engine as they could create spark and cause the battery to explode. It is imperative that you exercise extreme caution when dealing with batteries and electrical currents. Not only is the threat of electrocution real, so is the possibility of igniting the acidic fumes from the battery from a spark. Before attempting to jump-start a car, turn off all electrical equipment on both cars. This includes lights, radio, heater or air conditioning, DVD players, etc. Also, don't smoke or allow someone else to smoke near or around the car engines. Be sure you are wearing safety goggles before you attempt the jump-start. No portion of the vehicles should be touching when attempting to jump-start a car. There should be approximately 2 feet of space between the vehicles. Both cars should be in PARK or NEUTRAL and both engines should be off before connecting the jumper cables. It is also important to identify the positive and negative terminals on each battery. Some batteries have the positive (+) and negative (-) signs imprinted on the battery. While other batteries have the signs printed directly on the terminals, which may be covered with a removable, protective cap. Though the cap may also have the positive and negative signs on it, it is a good idea to make sure each cap has been returned to the correct terminal. You can remove the cap by prying it off and looking for the sign printed directly on the terminal. Also, never attempt to jump-start a car if either battery shows signs of corrosion, is cracked, or in any other way appears unsafe. One last thing, always follow the instructions for jumping a car exactly. There is only one way to connect and disconnect jumper cables and these steps must be followed in their proper order. OK, that was a lot to swallow. As promised, I have provided a list of all of the safety precautions I've just covered on page 24.

## JUMPER CABLE SAFETY PRECAUTIONS

- Consult your Owner's Manual for specific information on jump-starting your car.
- Remove all jewelry and any clothing with metal fasteners, zippers, etc.
- Keep all metal objects, such as tools, away from the battery and engine.
- Do not smoke or use open flames near the vehicles or battery.
- Wear safety goggles when working near batteries.
- Turn off all electrical equipment on both vehicles.
- Do not allow the vehicles to touch, leaving 2 feet of space between them.
- Place both vehicles in PARK or NEUTRAL, engage the Emergency Brake.
- Identify the positive (+) and negative (-) terminals for each vehicle.
- Check both batteries for signs of corrosion or damage that could make a jump unsafe.
- Always follow the instructions to connect and disconnect jumper cables exactly as they are listed.

Now that I have covered the safety measures, let's get down to business. For the purposes of this procedure I will use the words, 'Good' to describe the vehicle providing the jump and 'Bad' to describe the vehicle with the dead battery.

## USING JUMPER CABLES

1. Connect the Positive cable to the Positive terminal on the 'Bad' vehicle, ensuring that all safety precautions listed above have been met. (See Figure 6 for an example of proper jumper cable setup).

2. Connect the other end of the Positive cable to the Positive terminal on the 'Good' vehicle.

3. Connect the Negative cable to the Negative terminal on the 'Good' vehicle.

4. Connect the other end of the Negative cable to the Engine Block of the 'Bad' vehicle.

    a. Keep the cable away from the battery and other parts that will move when the vehicle is started.

    b. Do not connect the cable to the battery of the 'Bad' vehicle.

5. Step away from vehicles.

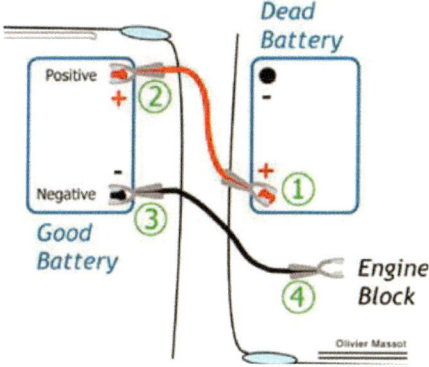

Figure 6 Jumper Cable Setup

**WARNING: Do not start engines until everyone has stepped away from the vehicles.**

- The owner of the 'Good' vehicle should start their vehicle's engine.
- Caution the owner not to 'rev' the engine.

6. Let the 'Good' engine idle for about 2 minutes.

7. Start the engine of the 'Bad' vehicle. If the 'Bad' vehicle starts, do not turn the engine off. It may take more than one try to start. Disconnect the cables in the proper order, if the 'Bad' vehicle does not start after 3 attempts.

8. Disconnect the jumper cables by reversing the order in which they were connected (as described above).

   - Do not allow the cables to touch each other when disconnecting.
   - Be careful of moving parts within the vehicle engines.

9. Remove the Negative cable from the Engine Block on the 'Bad' vehicle first.

10. Continue disconnecting the cables in the reverse order, ending with the Positive cable on the 'Bad' vehicle.

## Maintenance Log – Sample Sheet

### Maintenance Log – Sample Sheet

| Maintenance Task | Date Performed | Work Performed | Notes or Follow Up |
|---|---|---|---|
| Engine Oil Check | 10/18/2007 | Added one quart of oil | |
| Engine Oil Changed | 12/5/2007 | Oil changed, oil filter replaced | |
| Air Filter Check | | | |
| Tire Pressure Check | | | |
| Tire Tread Check | | | |
| Hoses and Belts Check | | | |
| Clean Wiper Blades | | | |
| Replace Wiper Blades | | | |
| Add Washer Fluid | | | |

# Glossary

**Air Filter** – pleated papery device that traps and filters the dust and debris from your engine or the air.

**Carburetor** – part of a combustible engine, device used to mix fuel and air within a vehicle engine to create ignition.

**Dipstick** – device inserted into a metal tube within the engine, used to read fluid level, as with engine oil and transmission fluid.

**Electronic Fuel Injection** – system that replaced the carburetor, controlled electronically by a computer within the engine, injects the fuel/air mixture into the engine to create ignition.

**Fuel Filter** – device within the fuel system used to filter debris and impurities from fuel.

**Fuel Injectors** – tubes or nozzles through which fuel is injected in the intake to mix with air during combustion.

**Fuel Line** – hose used to transport fuel through the fuel injection system.

**Fuel Pump** – the pump that regulates and distributes fuel from the fuel tank to the engine.

**Fuel Tank** – reservoir in which fuel is stored or held.

**Injection Nozzles** – tubes or nozzles through which fuel is injected.

**Intake Port** – passage within the cylinder head that directs the fuel/air mixture from the intake manifold's intake valve during the combustion process.

**Intake Valve** – part of the combustion process, valve within the cylinder head, allows the air and fuel to combine before being distributed to the fuel injectors.

**Multi-Port** – type of electronic fuel injection, the fuel/air mixture is performed in the intake port and distributed through individual fuel injectors to each cylinder.

**Oil Filler (cap)** – location in which engine oil is added, within the engine.

**Oil Pan** – reservoir within the engine where engine oil is held and drawn during combustion process.

**PSI** – abbreviation for Pounds per Square Inch. Used in reference to tire pressure.

**Serpentine Belt** – also known as a drive belt, single circular belt used to drive multiple engine parts and devices.

**Solenoid** – a mechanical device regulated by the electrical system within the fuel injection system, used in throttle body fuel injection systems.

**Throttle** – valve that regulates the flow of fuel in the cylinders.

**Tire Valve** – small device mounted in the tire rim used to measure tire pressure, and to add or remove air to tires.

**Valve Cap** – metal or plastic cap covering the tire valve.

# General references and resources

## *Book, Website, and Internet Sources*

- Jackson, Mary. 1989 and 1995. *The greaseless guide to car care*, Second Edition. Santa Fe, New Mexico: John Muir Publications.

- Monino, Juan. 2006. Tire Pressure Gauge. iStockphoto File Number: 2054193. http://www.istockphoto.com/file_closeup/?id=2054193&refnum=817038.

- Primrose Holdings, LLC. 1997- 2007. Maximum tire inflation image. http://www.tiresunlimited.bc.ca/images/tire.gif.

- Sclar, Deanna. 1999. *Auto Repair for Dummies*. IDG Books Worldwide.

- SmartTrac Computer Systems, Inc. 2000-2007. Serpentine belt image. http://tbn0.google.com/images?q=tbn:Zwqd-d1DlMaydM:http://www.familycar.com/classroom/Images/Engine.jpg.

- Sussman, Julie, and Stephanie Glakas-Tenet. 2005. *Dare to repair your car: a do-it-herself guide to maintenance, safety, minor fix-its, and talking shop.* USA: HarperCollins.

- Ubell, Alvin, Label Shulman, and Family Circle Magazine. 1983. Family Circle Winter Car Guide/Battery Setup. Jumper cable setup image. Accurate Building Inspectors. http://www.accuratebuilding.com/images/publications/family_circle/fc_winter_car_guide/battery_setup.jpg.

- 2005. Dodge Ram User Manual.

- 2007. http://images.google.com/imghp?tab=wi.

- 2007. http://www.powerblocktv.com/.

## Index

**—A—**
About this manual
  what it will *not* teach .. *See* Introduction
  what it will teach ........ *See* Introduction
**—E—**
Engine oil
  adding ................................................. 7
  engine oil ........................................... 7
  how much to add ............................... 7
  how often to check ............................ 7
  how to add ......................................... 7
  how to check ..................................... 7
  oil dipstick ......................................... 7
  oil filler cap ....................................... 7
  step-by-step instructions ................... 7
  when to add ...................................... 7
  when to check .................................... 7
Essentials
  air filter .............................................. 5
  engine oil ........................................... 5
  first-aid kit ......................................... 5
  gloves ................................................ 5
  jumper cables .................................... 5
  list of supplies ................................... 5
  Maintenance log ................................ 5
  Owner's manual ................................. 5
  pliers .................................................. 5
  protective goggles ............................. 5
  rags .................................................... 5
  screwdrivers ...................................... 5
  step-stool, short ladder ...................... 5
  tire gauge ........................................... 5
  washer fluid ....................................... 5
  wire brush .......................................... 5
Examples
  jumper cable setup .. *See* Jumper cables
  maximum psi ......................... *See* Tires

  serpentine belt ....... *See* Hoses and belts
  tire gauge ............................... *See* Tires
  tire valve ................................ *See* Tires
Extras
  jumper cables .................................. 22
  more essentials .*See* Jumper cables, *See* Windshield wipers
  windshield wipers ............................ 20
**—F—**
Fuel system
  air filter ............................................ 10
  carburetor ........................................ 10
  changing air filter ............................ 10
  checking air filter ............................ 10
  combustion chamber ....................... 10
  electronic fuel injection ................... 10
  fuel injection system ....................... 10
  fuel injectors ................................... 10
  fuel lines ......................................... 10
  fuel pump ........................................ 10
  fuel tank ........................................... 10
  gas tank ......................... *See* fuel tank
  injection nozzles ........ *See* throttle body
  intake port ..................... *See* multi-port
  intake valve ................... *See* multi-port
  multi-port ........................................ 10
  Owner's Manual ............................. 10
  solenoid .................... *See* throttle body
  step-by-step instructions ................. 10
  throttle body ................................... 10
**—H—**
Hoses and belts
  belts ................................................ 17
  clamps ............................................. 17
  drive belt ................. *See* serpentine belt
  hoses ............................................... 17

performing the Look-Listen check - serpentine belt and hoses............... 17
performing the Touch-Feel check - hoses.............................................. 17
performing the Touch-Feel check - serpentine belt ............................... 17
preventative maintenance................. 17
replacing........................................... 17
safety................................................ 17
serpentine belt ................................. 17
step-by-step instructions .................. 17
step-stool, ladder ............................. 17

—I—

Introduction
about this manual ............................... 1
engine bay ........................................... 1
oil dipstick location ............................ 1
oil filler cap location ........................... 1
Owner's Manual .................................. 1
washer fluid location ........................... 1
what this manual will *not* teach........... 1
what this manual will teach................. 1

—J—

Jumper cables
"Good' battery ................................... 22
acidic fumes ...................................... 22
'Bad' battery...................................... 22
battery............................................... 22
caution when using........................... 22
connecting cables ............................. 22
disconnecting cables ........................ 22
electrical equipment ......................... 22
electrocution..................................... 22
identifying negative terminal ........... 22
identifying positive terminal ............ 22
list of safety precautions .................. 22
metal and the battery ........................ 22
Owner's Manual ............................... 22
preparing to use .......... *See* list of safety precautions
purchasing ........................................ 22
safety ................................................ 22
safety goggles................................... 22
setup ................................................. 22

step-by-step instructions ...................22

—L—

Locating parts
air filter.. *See* Fuel system, step-by-step instructions
engine bay .................. *See* Introduction
maximum psi information.......*See* Tires
oil dipstick............................................1, 7
oil filler cap ............... 7, *See* Engine oil
serpentine belt ....... *See* Hoses and belts
tire gauge................................*See* Tires
tire valve.................................*See* Tires
washer fluid......*See* Windshield wipers

—M—

Maintenance Log
sample sheet......................................27

—O—

Owner's Manual ............... *See* Engine oil, Essentials, Fuel system, Introduction, Jumper cables, Tires

—T—

Tires
adding air ..........................................12
alignment...........................................12
assessing tire wear and tear...............12
Certification Label ............................12
checking tire pressure .......................12
cold air check ............ *See* checking tire pressure
driving conditions .............................12
gas stations and air .........*See* adding air
life of tires ..........................*See* rotation
Maintenance log................................12
objects embedded..............................12
'one cent' check .... *See* performing 'one cent' check
Owner's Manual ................................12
pattern of rotation........ *See* tire rotation
penny check . *See* performing 'one cent' check
performing the 'one cent' check ........12
proper inflation..................................12
psi......................................................12
rotation ..............................................12

Jessy Patterson

31

safety ................................................. 12
steering .............................................. 12
step-by-step instructions .................. 12
tire balancing ..................................... 12
tire gauge ........................................... 12
tire pressure requirement .................. 12
tire valve ............................................ 12
tire walls ............................................ 12
tread ................................................... 12
tread assessment ................................ 12
tread wear .......................................... 12
valve cap ........................................... 12
visual assessment .............................. 12
wear patterns ..................................... 12

## —W—

What you will need
   getting started ........................................ 5
   list of supplies ................. See Essentials
   the right tools ........................................ 5
Windshield wipers
   adding washer fluid ............................. 20
   cleaning ............................................... 20
   replacing .............................................. 20
   washer fluid ......................................... 20
   what you need to know when buying 20
   where to buy ........................................ 20
   wiper blades ........................................ 20
   wipers .................................................. 20

Made in the USA
Lexington, KY
04 January 2016